ESSENTIAL COUNTRY
Guitar Technique

by Michael Fath

Cover art by Levin Pfeufer

Recording Credits: Micheal Fath, Guitar

Cherry Lane Music Company
Educational Director/Project Supervisor: Susan Poliniak
Director of Publications: Mark Phillips

ISBN 1-57560-724-7

Copyright © 2005 Cherry Lane Music Company
International Copyright Secured   All Rights Reserved

The music, text, design and graphics in this publication are protected by copyright law. Any duplication or transmission,
by any means, electronic, mechanical, photocopying, recording or otherwise, is an infringement of copyright.

Visit our website at www.cherrylane.com

Table of Contents

Introduction 4
About the Author 5

Bluegrass–Style Banjo Rolls 6
Solo: Earl the Pearl 8

Travis Picking 10
Solo: Merle, Another Pearl 13

Scales 15
Solo: Step in Time 17

Violin–Style Arpeggios 19
Solo: Sweep Away 21

Fingerstyle Arpeggios 23
Solo: Hybrid–Hi Melody 25

Double Stops 27
Solo: Double Your Pleasure 29

Pedal Steel Bends 31
Solo: Bend Me, Shape Me 33

Open–String Techniques 35
Solo: Open Your Mind 36

Seventh Chords 38
Solo: Seventh Heaven 40

Scale/Rhythm Combinations 42
Solo: Rhythm and Grooves 44

More Seventh Chords 46
Solo: Transition Condition 48

Country Swing 49
Solo: Dance to the Music 50

Guitar Notation Legend 52

Introduction

Today's premium country guitarist needs to be an even better player than the hot picker of yesterday. He or she needs not only to possess those licks that have previously graced the various chart-topping records of our country superstars, but also have the skills necessary to stay ahead of the game. This means that the greatest players of tomorrow must have command of the standard country pickin' techniques we have all learned to love and, in addition, have under their fingers rockabilly, bluegrass, R&B, progressive rock, jazz, and even classical techniques!

If you are unfamiliar with but interested in learning country guitar technique, this book can have an immediate impact on developing those basic but essential skills. If you are already an accomplished country guitarist, this book can motivate and influence you into becoming an even greater player.

TRACK 01

Note: Track 1 contains tuning pitches.

About the Author

At last count, northern Virginia–based guitarist Michael Fath had 22 instrumental CDs to his credit. His recordings are in styles as diverse as fusion jazz (*The Chase Is On*, Shenandoah Records, 2004), progressive rock (*Sonic Tapestries*, R.E.D. Inc. Records, 1990), roots acoustic (*Songs for Marie*, Independent, 1998), progressive country fusion (*Country Squire*, CUE Records, 1995), and straight-ahead solo jazz (*In My Life*, Shenandoah Records, 2003).

Michael Fath

Michael has spent years headlining concerts with his groups and also as a soloist in venues throughout the U.S. and Europe (the Kennedy Center in Washington, D.C., the Marquee in London, etc.). He has been nominated for the guitarist of the year award by various guitar and music magazines (*Guitar Magazine*, for one) and music associations, and has won several of these awards. Michael has guitars hanging in various Hard Rock Cafés around the country, has sponsorships and endorsements from a wide variety of companies (Fender, D'Angelico, and Gibson, to name just a few), and has written monthly columns for several guitar magazines in the U.S. and Europe.

Mike has a fusion trio that plays regularly, and his nine-piece horn project, Le Jazz, recently released its debut CD, *The Chase Is On*. Formerly a frequent performer at some of the best venues in Nashville, Michael now saves his best country licks for his own recordings and other projects. He can be contacted through his website at www.michaelfath.com.

Bluegrass-Style Banjo Rolls

An essential technique for any country guitarist is the simulation of those wonderful banjo rolls that permeate bluegrass and mountain music. For years, Earl Scruggs' banjo lines have caught our attention, and this particular technique has been a mainstay of Nashville studio legends such as Albert Lee and Brent Mason.

A *hybrid picking* (using a pick and fingers) technique is essential to playing these melodies. The right-hand fingering is notated in this book as follows: *p* for either your thumb or the pick held by your thumb and index finger, *m* for the middle finger, and *a* for the ring finger. Typically, banjo players wear metal picks on their right-hand thumbs, index fingers, and middle fingers—this is how the term *claw hammer* originated. Unless you are one of the small percentage of guitar players who use a *thumbpick* (a pick worn on the right-hand thumb), the hybrid picking technique is the only way to mimic the banjo sound properly.

Here is a lick that uses the open G string to simulate a banjo in open G. Observe that the melody is basically a three-finger/three-note combination against a four-beat rhythm (in this case, sets of four 16th notes). Practice this very slowly and concentrate on creating even tones and volumes between the pick and fingers. This first exercise is at a very slow tempo on the CD so you can get used to the feel.

TRACK 02

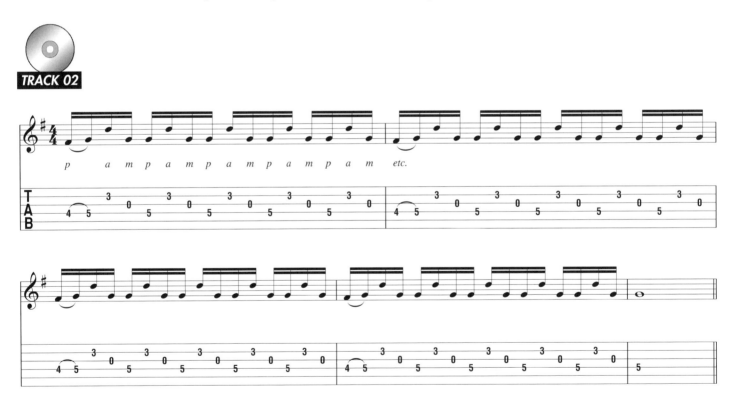

Here's the same lick at full tempo (fast!) and with a slight note change.

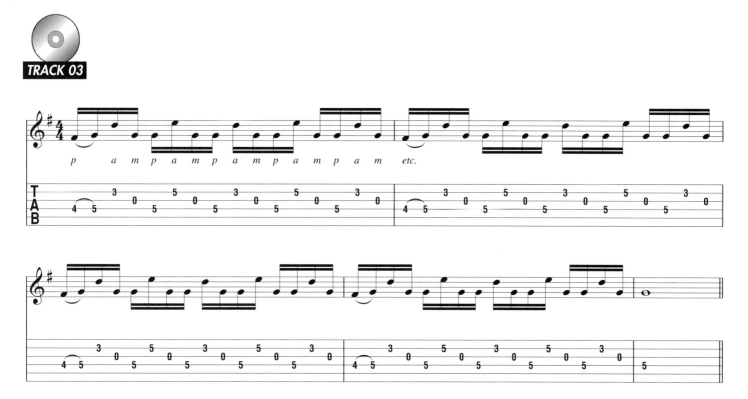

This next exercise uses a different inversion of the G major triad with one note (A) of the G major pentatonic scaled added. Start the fretting with your ring finger handling the slide, and the rest will fall into place. Observe that there are no open strings this time—this idea is *movable,* so it can be played in other places on the fretboard in different keys.

Also, note that from here on out, you'll be presented with both full-tempo (fast!) and slow versions of every example on the CD.

TRACK 04   TRACK 05
Slow Demo

Here's another movable idea in G major. This one requires a little more left-hand movement for the added chromatic tones, but it's a valuable pattern to have under your fingers. For the fretting, begin with your index finger and slide into the barre at the 12th fret. For the ascending notes on the B and G strings, start out with your middle and ring fingers for the A and C, respectively, and then switch to your ring finger and pinky for the rest.

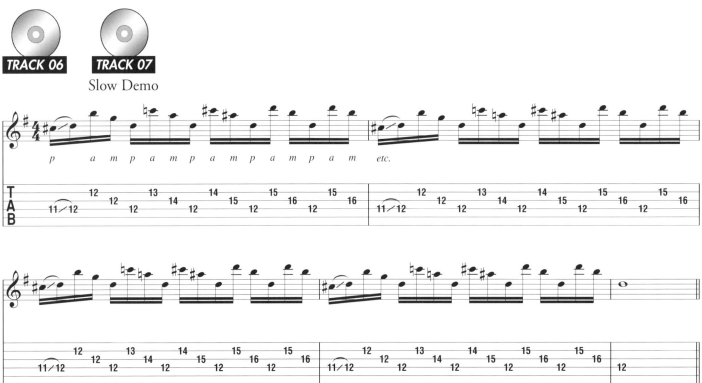

Solo: Earl the Pearl

This solo, a melodic technical study, incorporates several of the banjo roll techniques to cover all of the changes in a typical 12-bar country/bluegrass–style progression. One very important concept to grasp here is the visual memorization of these different chord forms and positions, so that once you've mastered the banjo roll techniques, it will be easy to improvise through other changes, no matter what chords are involved.

The right-hand fingering is the same as in the exercises. For the left hand, in measure 4 pull off with the middle finger and then go into an index-finger barre. The next measure has a slide into another index-finger barre. Begin measure 9 with a ring-finger slide, and the rest of that bar will fall into place.

Remember that speed is, at first, the least important point. What is necessary is a very precise attack of each and every note.

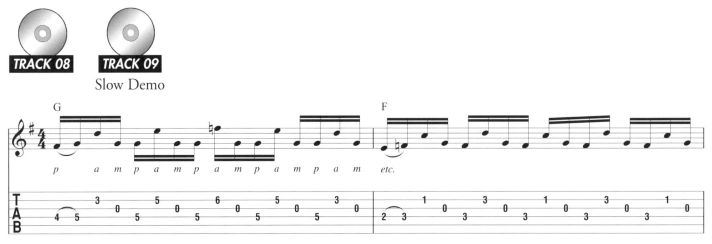

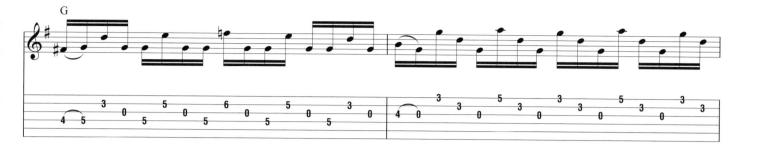

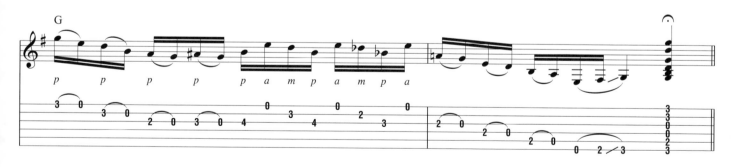

Travis Picking

Another essential technique for the modern-day country guitarist is *Travis picking*, named after the legendary guitarist Merle Travis. This style involves playing a rhythmic bass pattern and an accompanying melody line at the same time. Travis picking has always been a core ingredient of the rockabilly style, with its basic solo and rhythmic structures based almost entirely upon this style of playing.

While Merle didn't exactly invent this technique (he learned it from Mose Roger and Ike Everly, father of the Everly Brothers), he certainly deserves the credit for refining and popularizing it. He was also one of the first players who believed that the guitar could and should be a lead instrument. The list of guitar players who Merle influenced directly is a virtual star roster of country, bluegrass, rockabilly, and popular music: Chet Atkins, Doc Watson, Jerry Reed, Albert Lee, George Harrison, Eddie Cochran, Duane Eddy, Carl Perkins, Scotty Moore, James Burton, Marcel Dadi, Brian Setzer, and many more.

Although Merle used a thumbpick (most likely a habit picked up from his banjo-playing father), it is not necessary to use one yourself. The hybrid picking technique can be employed.

Below is a simple exercise based on an open E chord. It is essential to get the bass pattern down first; all of the bass notes are played with pick downstrokes and should be practiced very slowly and deliberately when you're just starting out. Play the melody with your right-hand middle finger. As you grow as a country player, you'll find that with more difficult melodies and double stops you may also need to use your ring finger. As far as the left hand goes, fret the 4th-string E with your middle finger, the 2nd-string C♯ with your ring finger, and the 1st-string G with your pinky.

Notice that for these examples in cut time, you get *two* measures of count-off clicks, and each of the clicks represents a half note.

Here's an extremely useful E7 and D7 chord melody exercise with a slightly more complex bass pattern. This can be transposed to any key and requires both your right-hand middle and ring fingers to play the melody. For the left hand, use the standard C7 chord shape fingering.

TRACK 12   **TRACK 13**
              Slow Demo

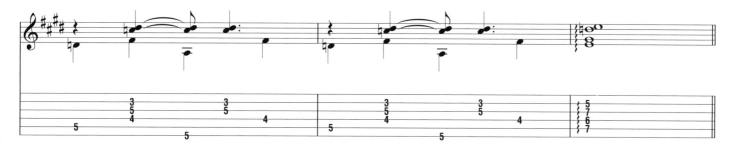

Below is a more complex melody exercise using an open E major chord. Once the bass patterns are really in your fingers—you're not consciously thinking about them—your melodic potential can be unleashed!

TRACK 14 **TRACK 15**
Slow Demo

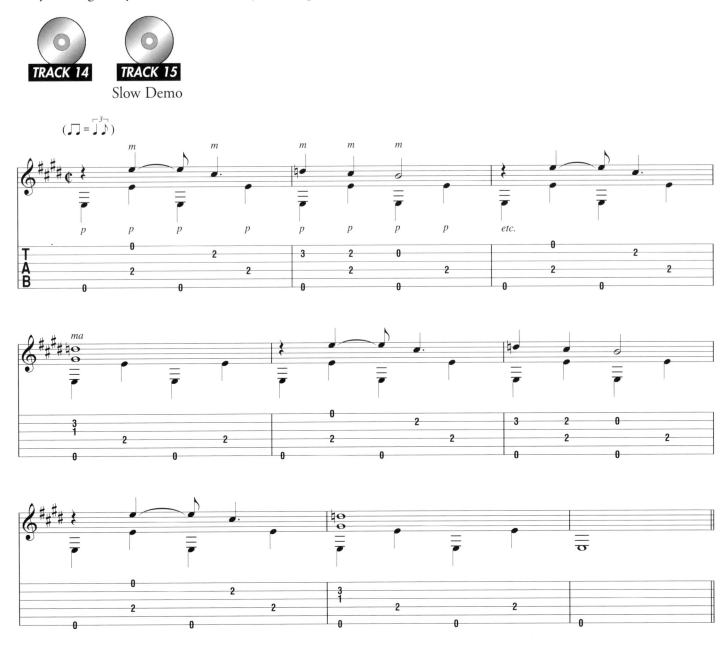

Solo: Merle, Another Pearl

This solo utilizes several Travis-picking techniques to cover the changes in a typical 12-bar progression. Both the bass patterns and the melodic patterns are equally important. When you're first starting out with Travis picking, it's necessary to separate your thought processes for each of these.

Similar to "Earl the Pearl," this particular study ends with a hot rockabilly blues–style lick, finishing with an E6 chord that sounds very appropriate in this setting.

TRACK 16   TRACK 17
Slow Demo

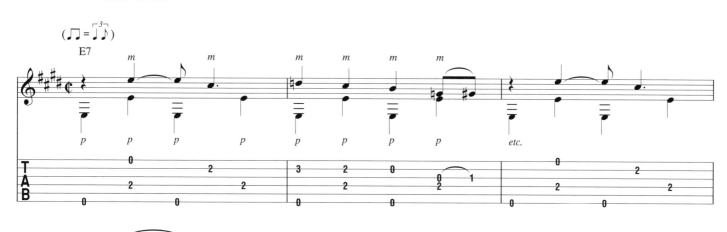

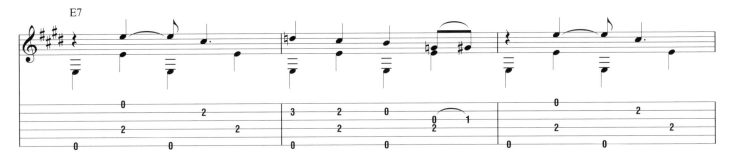

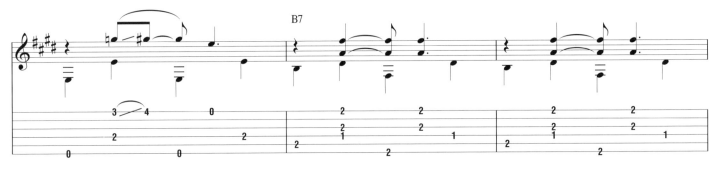

Scales

Country music's charm can be found in its simplicity, and the harmonies of country music are fairly simple by nature. You generally won't find complex harmonies, such as the altered dominant 7th chords found in jazz styles like be-bop and swing, or the modal intricacies of jazz/rock fusion. This does not mean that the solos and rhythmic variations found in country music are easy. In fact, quite the opposite is true—solos with simple three-chord progressions require a great deal of creativity.

The scales used in this style are mainly the minor pentatonic (sometimes with a ♭5 to form the blues scale), the major pentatonic (with a minor 3rd added for added country flavor), and the dominant 7th scale (a major scale with a ♭7). But it is essential to know when and how to add the right chromatic notes to embellish these three scales. We'll explore a few licks using this very idea in just a moment.

This first exercise should sound very familiar—it's a stock country lick that combines the A major pentatonic scale (with the added ♭3) with the A Mixolydian mode and dominant 7th scales. Pay close attention to the hammer-ons and pull-offs, as this phrase sounds most effective when these are combined with precise alternate picking.

TRACK 18   TRACK 19
            Slow Demo

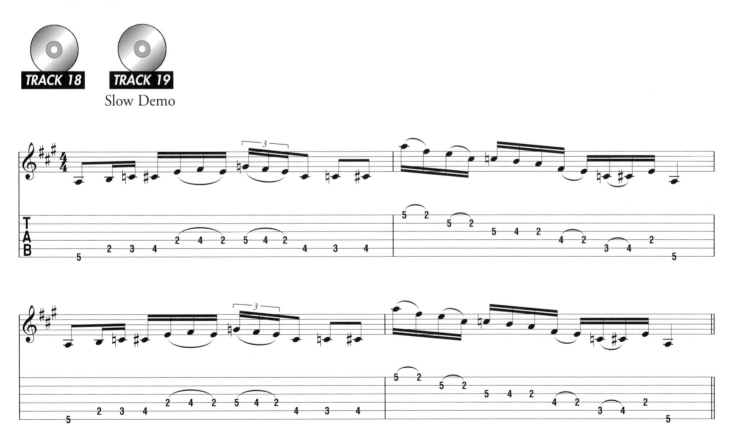

Here's another dominant 7th scale, but this time filled in with chromatic notes to give it a lot of zip. What makes this even more melodic is the blues lick that finishes each phrase.

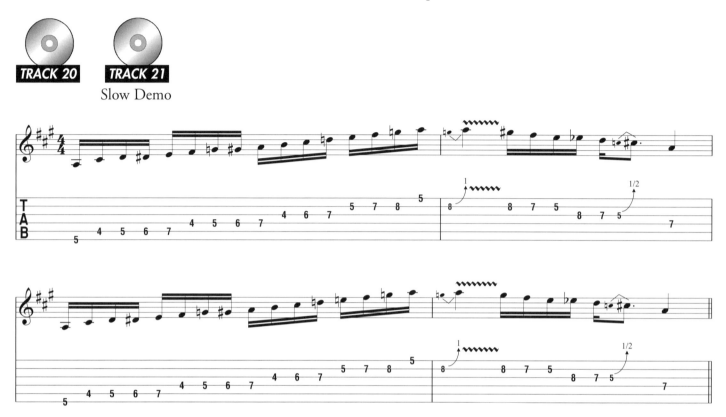

TRACK 20   **TRACK 21**
                 Slow Demo

This exercise combines the hybrid picking technique with alternate picking and slurring to create that chicken-pickin' sound. If you practice all three of these licks very slowly at first, paying complete attention to detail, they will sound great when played up to speed.

TRACK 22   **TRACK 23**
                 Slow Demo

Solo: Step in Time

This solo explores the aforementioned scale ideas, using the 12-bar format to frame these types of hot country pickin' and combined hybrid- and alternate-picking techniques. Try to make the visual "connection" with
these scale melodies and their respective chords—this is essential to improvising later on! Play this solo slowly and cleanly at first, and gradually work the tempo up to speed.

TRACK 24   TRACK 25
             Slow Demo

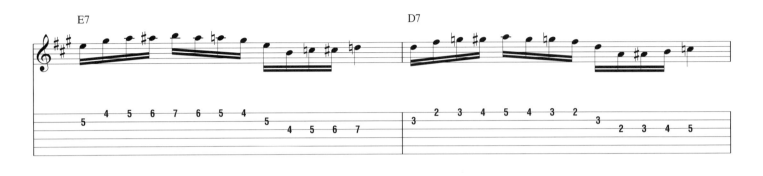

Violin-Style Arpeggios

I've always been a huge fan of classical music. Bach, Mozart, Beethoven, Paganini—I could go on and on. I particularly enjoy composers such as Ravel, Debussy, Copland, and Gershwin because they were part of the musical transition into 20th-century styles and contributed in different ways to a uniquely American style of music—jazz!

In listening to many well-known classical pieces, you cannot help but notice certain kinds of soaring violin melodies that define chord changes. These are arpeggios, and although they can be played on any instrument, the violin has the range and speed capabilities to maximize their potential.

Years ago while listening to some of my favorite violinists, I noticed that they would play downbow for certain series of notes and upbow for others. I got the idea to simulate this motion with a pick, using downstrokes for some series of notes and upstrokes for others in a "sweeping" fashion—hence *sweep-picking*. No, I did not invent this technique, but I created it for myself and have had amazing results.

The marriage of classical and country music is not a new one. One of the very best examples of a musician exemplifying the best of both idioms is the violinist Mark O'Connor, whose skills have graced countless country and some classical recordings.

This first exercise combines a C9 arpeggio with a country scale ending. It is very important to use your blues and country scale ideas with these arpeggios, as otherwise they'll sound too "thought out" and theoretical as opposed to improvised. Pay very close attention to the pick strokes, because this whole concept relies on very smooth down and up motions coordinated exactly with the left-hand fingerings.

TRACK 26   TRACK 27
              Slow Demo

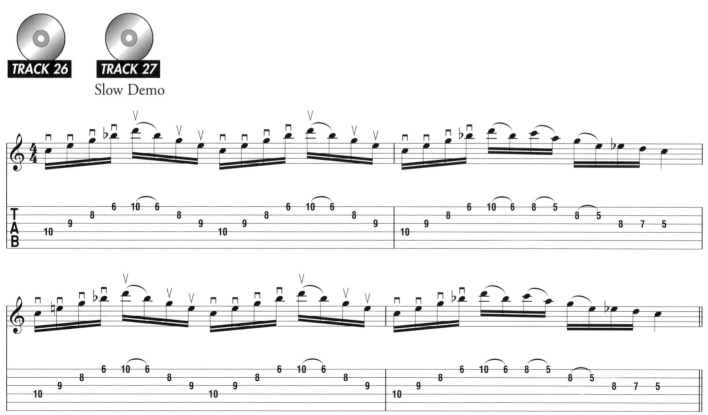

This next exercise combines a C major arpeggio in a different fretboard position with those familiar country-sounding chromatic passages.

TRACK 28   **TRACK 29**
                 Slow Demo

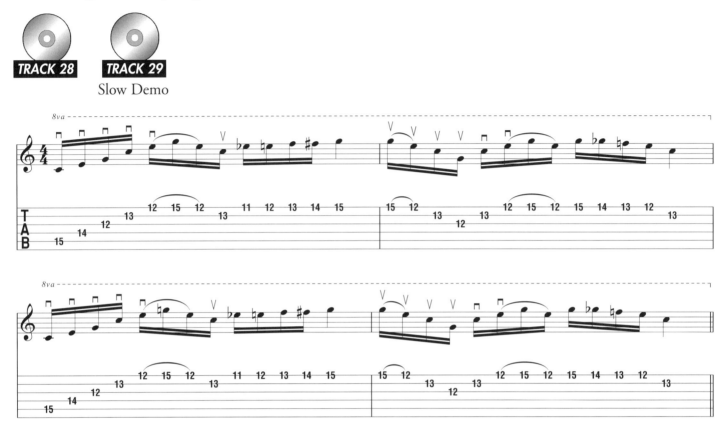

Here's yet another C major arpeggio, this time with the familiar barre chord shape and an added bluesy finish.

TRACK 30   **TRACK 31**
                 Slow Demo

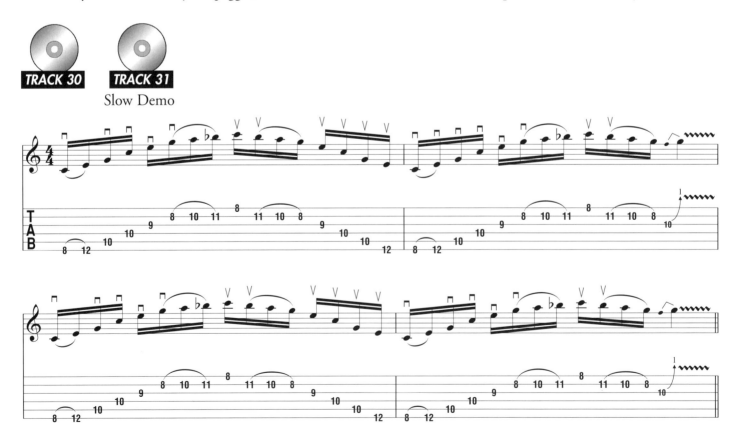

Solo: Sweep Away

This solo explores the arpeggio technique, combined with a modern touch and enough country scale picking to make it legitimate. These arpeggios have to be played very slowly and accurately before you can even think about playing them up to tempo. If you cannot hear every note that you are playing, then you may be trying to play too quickly.

TRACK 32   TRACK 33
Slow Demo

Violin-Style Arpeggios *cont.*

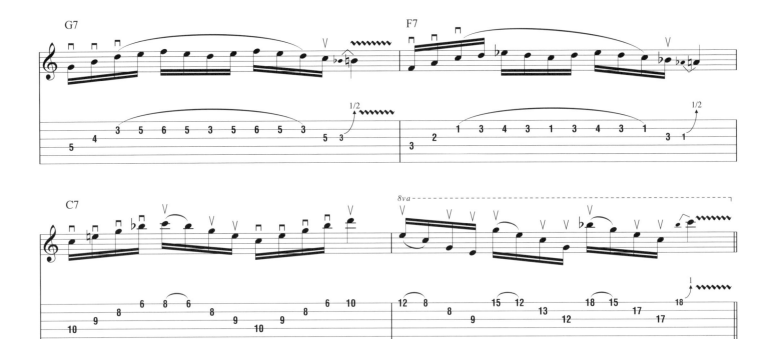

Fingerstyle Arpeggios

My philosophy has always been to seek out the obvious and not so obvious advantages to any particular technique and maximize its use. For one, there are distinct advantages to fingerstyle playing. In light of that, here is the arpeggio again—but this time played with hybrid picking.

This first exercise is an ear-catching descending and ascending pattern in E major. It is very important to play this phrase cleanly and with power, as the separation of the notes is essential. Try to visualize the chord patterns that make up these arpeggio sequences, as this can enhance your ability to improvise with this technique.

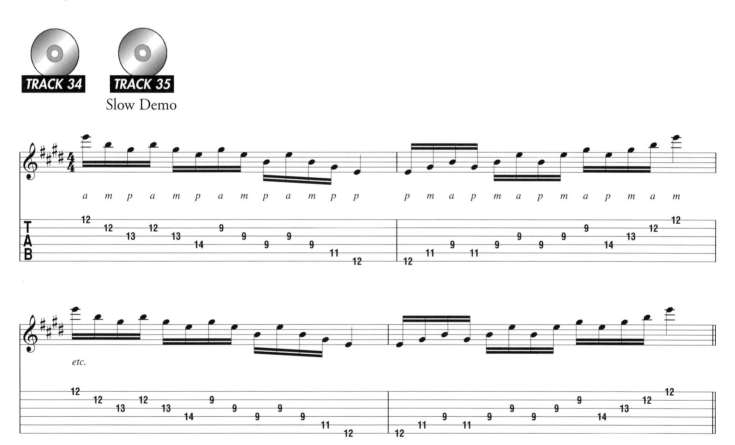

Here's an arpeggio lick using a pedal tone, which is a technique that employs a repeated note below or above other melodic activity. It is very important that all of the notes here are of equal volume—this is sometimes difficult to accomplish with the hybrid picking technique. This exercise really shows the advantage of using fingers to play pedal tones, as a pick-only approach would make it difficult to keep everything up to speed with these string-skipping phrases. By the way, play this one in 4th position.

TRACK 36   **TRACK 37**
Slow Demo

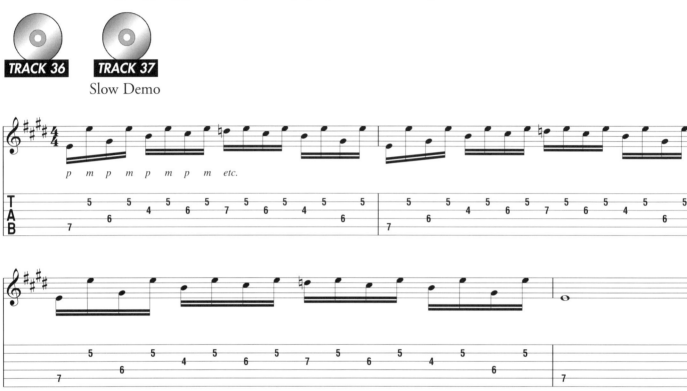

This exercise shows how you can play over chord changes with minimal left-hand movement. It is very important that each and every note is equal in volume whether it's being picked, plucked, or pulled-off.

TRACK 38   **TRACK 39**
Slow Demo

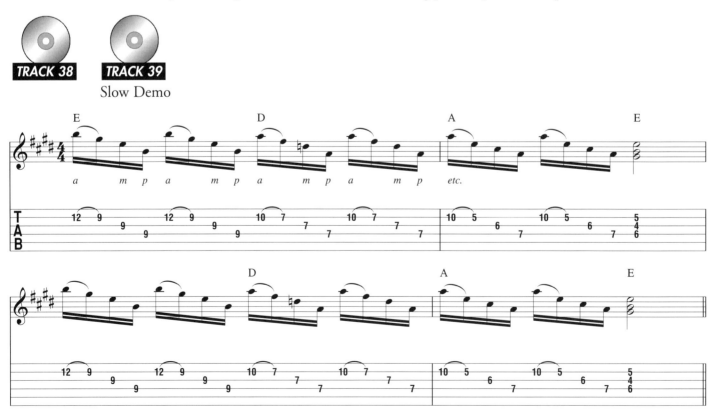

Solo: Hybrid-Hi Melody

The hybrid picking approach is especially useful for country players using clean tones as opposed to, say, rock players using distortion—although if executed precisely, arpeggios can sound impressive in any situation! Remember that any technique is useful if applied wisely. In most instances, this means melodically.

In order to give you an extreme workout with the hybrid picking technique applied to arpeggio playing, I kept this entire solo in arpeggio form. In normal situations, you would want to combine this approach with other melodic techniques (blues scales, double stops, etc.) to keep your solos from sounding too "formal."

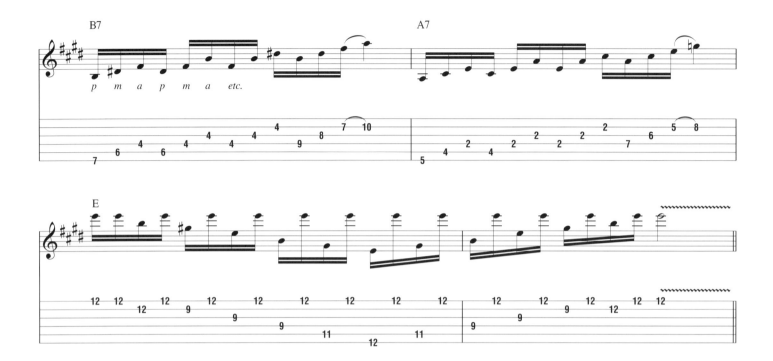

Double Stops

I have been a fan of bluegrass music, especially instrumentals, for as far back as I can remember. I listen close-ly to what the guitarists play, of course, but I also find myself paying closer and closer attention to what the mandolin, fiddle, and banjo players are doing, as I strive to be supremely innovative when it comes to my own guitar style. This is how I learned to play most of my banjo licks. I also look to the mandolin lines quite a bit, but what's especially intriguing for me is the double stop technique that bluegrass fiddle players use.

This first exercise is a major pentatonic/country scale–based riff that starts out slowly with eighth notes and ends in a flurry of 16ths. It is essential that your alternate pick strokes attack each of these double stops very evenly, as you must play "through" both notes as if they were one.

TRACK 42   TRACK 43
Slow Demo

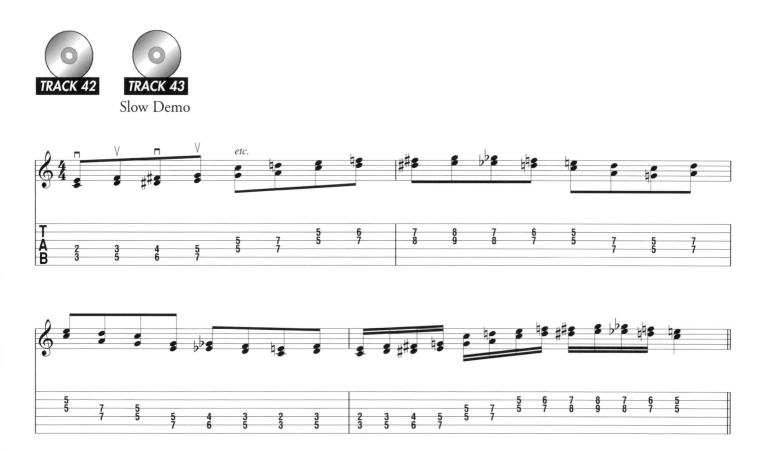

Double Stops *cont.*

This next exercise combines a hybrid-picked arpeggio in quarter note double stops with a blues-based alternate-picked ending.

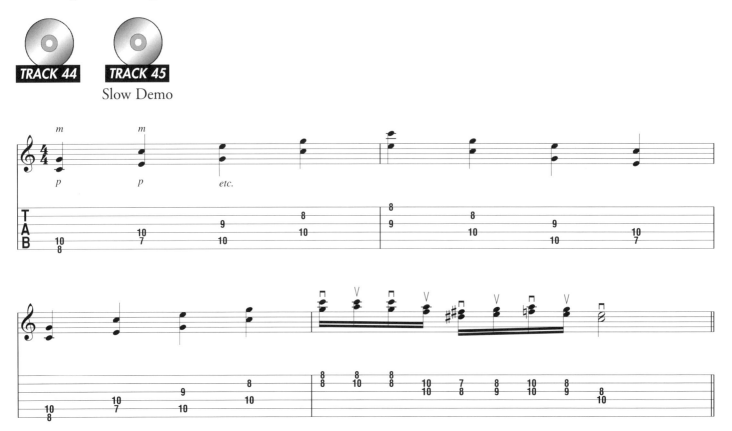

This lick utilizes both hybrid and alternate picking and is based on a familiar country sound.

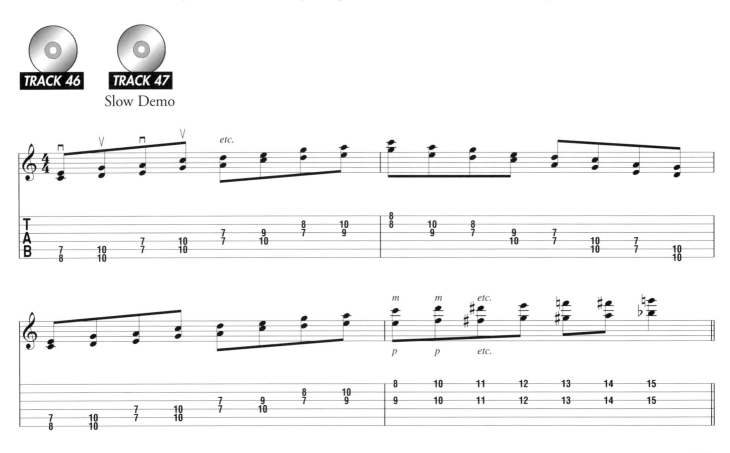

Solo: Double Your Pleasure

For this solo, I used chord changes that sound stylistically bluegrass. I also added some single-note lines to make it interesting and a blistering sweep-picked arpeggio at the end to make it memorable. Good luck with this one—you'll need it!

TRACK 48   TRACK 49
Slow Demo

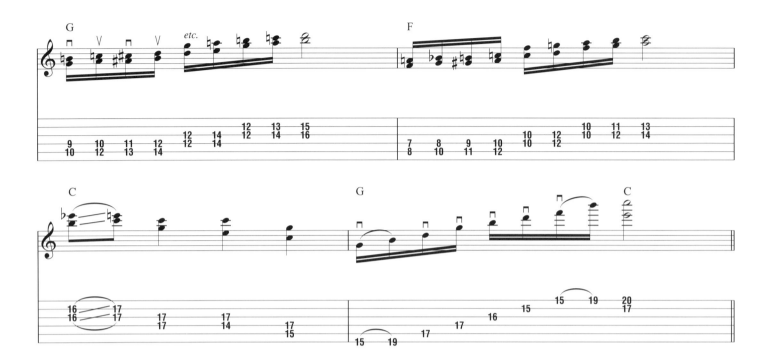

Pedal Steel Bends

Anyone who has heard—or, better yet, played with—a good pedal steel player knows exactly how cool their licks can be. There is something very silky about all of those bent notes. While it is true that steel players use pedals, knee levers, and slide bars to get their sound, it is possible to simulate this on an electric guitar. It takes very good left-hand finger independence and strength coupled with an even better ear to detect the subtle pitch differences that can make or break this technique. When you get beyond the initial stages of this type of playing, you can use your volume knob to enhance the pedal steel effect to an even greater degree.

One of the great masters of this guitar technique is Jerry Donahue of the infamous Hellecasters. He can make you believe that he is actually playing pedal steel guitar. The fabulous Albert Lee fits this bill as well.

Below is one of the most basic yet widely used and effective pedal steel licks I've played or heard to date. The right-hand technique for this one is hybrid picking. As for your left hand, watch your pitch on those bends. It's important to note that these licks won't work well on guitars with floating tremolo systems, as stretching one string will cause the others to go out of tune. A guitar with a blocked off bridge (such as a Telecaster) will produce the best results.

TRACK 50   TRACK 51
Slow Demo

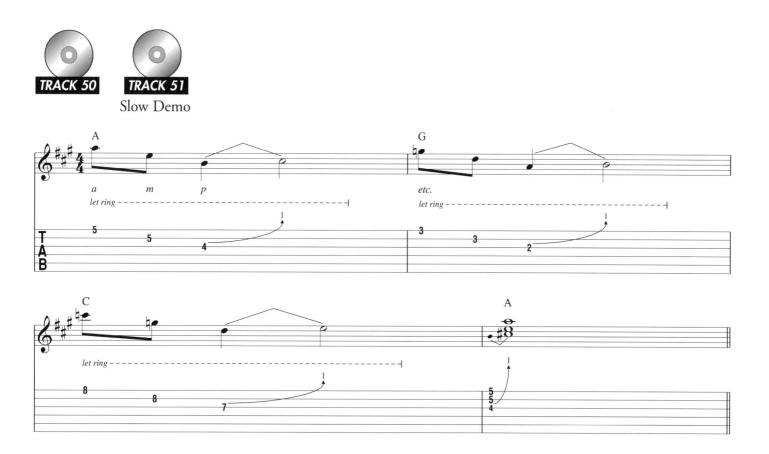

Here is another approach using open strings and lower notes.

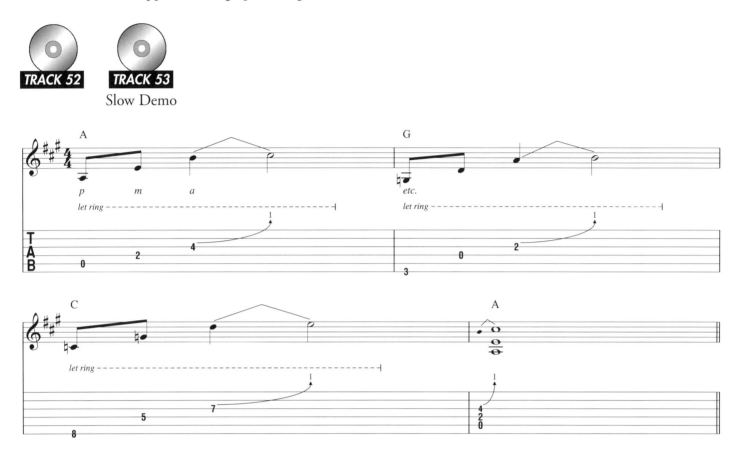

This exercise uses the same A–G–C–A chord sequence with a few added 6ths.

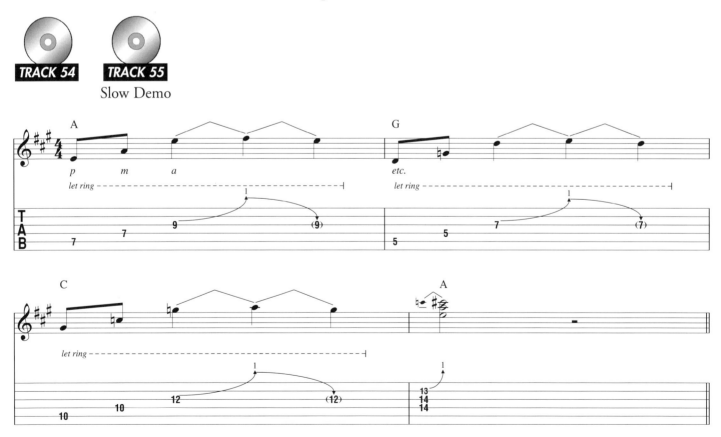

Solo: Bend Me, Shape Me

You've probably realized by now that this technique is much harder than it seems, which is why it is absolutely necessary to start off slowly. I trust that you will find this section's solo both challenging and rewarding.

This follows the familiar 12-bar format and includes basic major chord changes that sound stylistically country. I also incorporated some single-note lines to help you work on the transitions from playing scale licks to playing steel licks. Note that the chord at the end requires a great deal of left-hand finger control and accuracy.

TRACK 56   **TRACK 57**
             Slow Demo

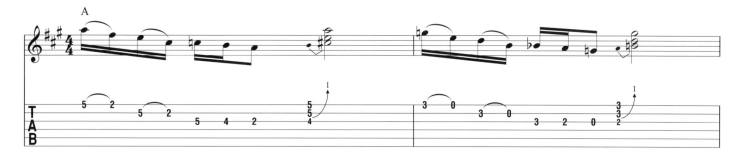

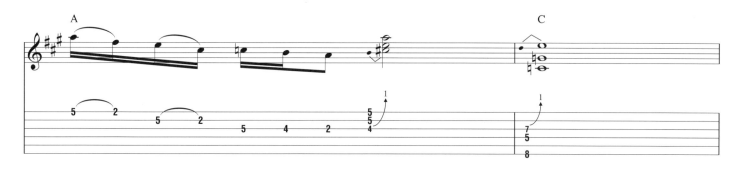

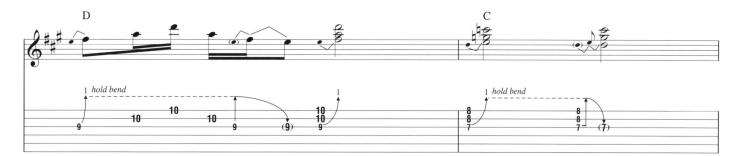

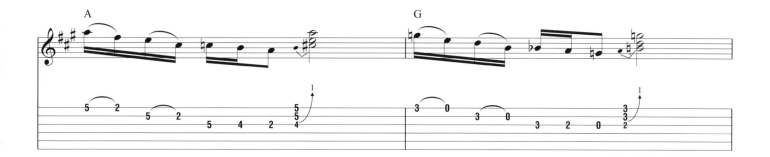

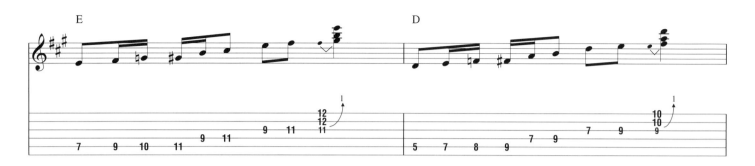

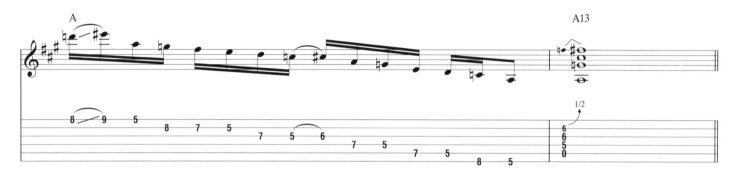

Open-String Techniques

Since most country guitar soloing is done with very clean tones, it is sometimes necessary to create sustain through means other than distortion (which doesn't really serve this type of music well). One sure-fire method of creating sustain is to use open-string notes along with fretted ones in arpeggios and scales to create an "over ring." When an open string is vibrating while a fretted note on another string is being played, you can get a sort of natural delay effect that can greatly enhance those clean tones. This is not an easy thing to do, often because many licks cannot be transposed into other keys and still contain open strings. Nevertheless, this can be a great technique where it is possible.

This first exercise uses the major pentatonic scale—every country guitarist's main weapon. Use the hybrid picking technique to maximize your efficiency.

Here is a cool lick that uses two open strings to support the scale pattern. This has to be played with equal attention to both of the open strings for optimum results.

Last but not least, here is a very hot bluesy riff that has a non-standard ending. Remember that originality is the key to life in music.

TRACK 62   **TRACK 63**
                Slow Demo

Solo: Open Your Mind

This solo uses basic major and 7th chords that sound stylistically bluesy/country. Your hybrid picking chops need to be in top form to execute some of these licks. As always, play slowly at first, and always very precisely—make sure you hear each and every note.

TRACK 64   **TRACK 65**
                Slow Demo

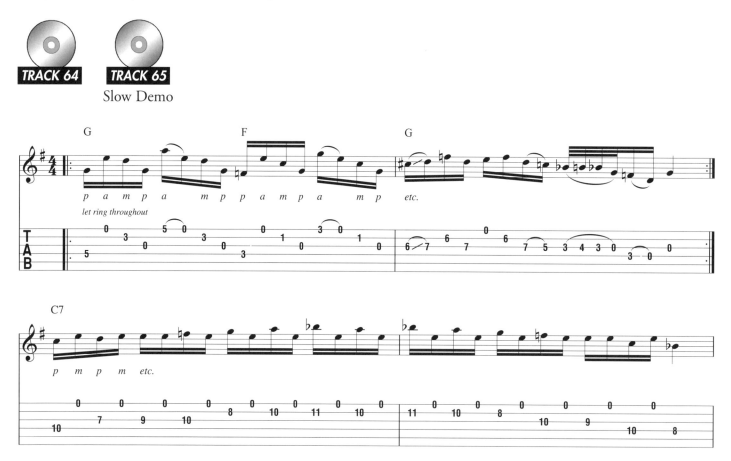

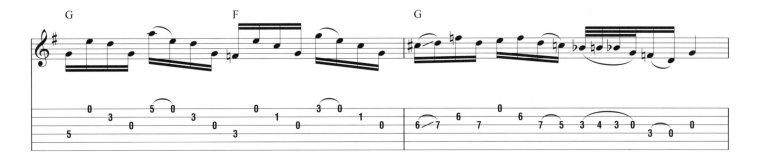

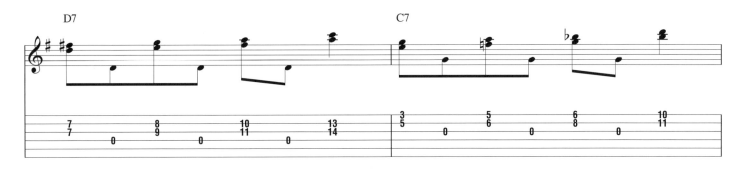

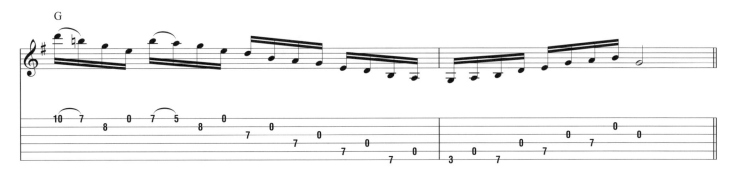

Seventh Chords

Simply put, the better your knowledge of chords, the better guitarist you will be—and I'm not talking about just rhythm playing. Most melodic phrases and solo licks are chord-based. Almost all country music compositions are based on the I–IV–V progression, and dominant 7th harmonies are often utilized.

Below are fretboard diagrams of the four versions (root plus the three inversions) of the A7 chord. Learn these shapes, as they can be moved to different positions on the fretboard to be played in different keys.

A7

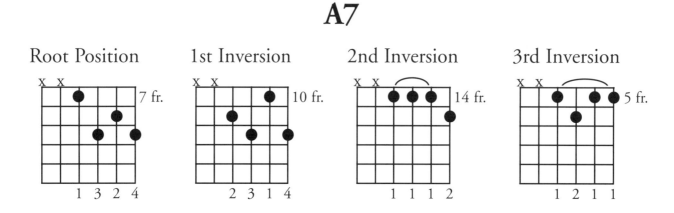

Root Position   1st Inversion   2nd Inversion   3rd Inversion

Either pluck or strum through these chords and make sure that each of the notes sounds clean and clear. Also, notice where the root note (A) is in each of the inversions.

TRACK 66   TRACK 67
Slow Demo

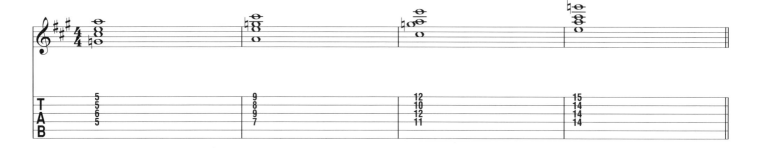

This next exercise takes the same chord forms at half the note durations (twice the pace).

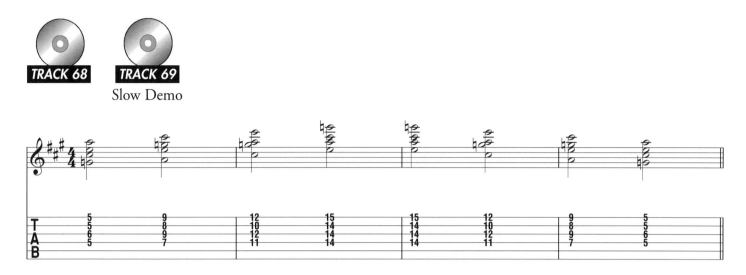

This last exercise involves a hybrid picking approach to playing these forms as arpeggios.

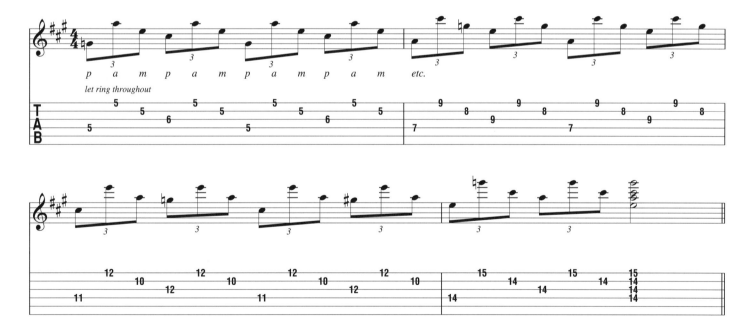

Solo: Seventh Heaven

This section's solo is a unique way to play through the I–IV–V changes of a country/blues 12-bar progression. The chords and melodies very smoothly and seamlessly "melt" into each other. Note that I used the sweep picking technique, but you may want to fingerpick or hybrid pick for different feels and sounds. When you're first starting out with this solo, play it slowly enough to really learn the chord forms and hear the changes.

TRACK 72   TRACK 73
Slow Demo

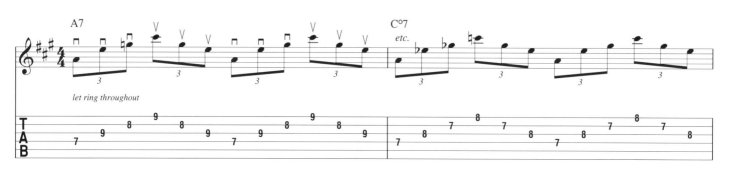

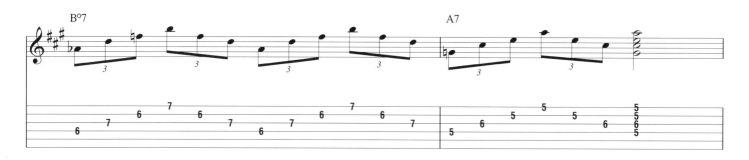

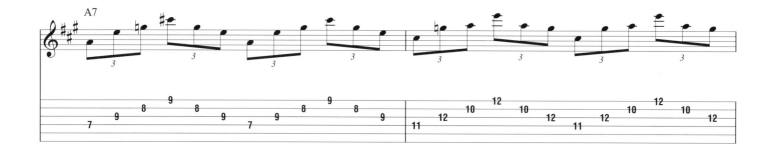

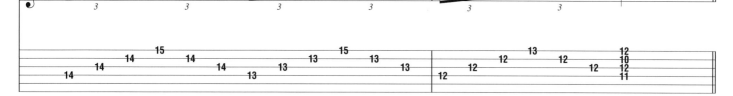

Scale/Rhythm Combinations

Popular opinion states that there's rhythm guitar and lead guitar, and never the twain shall meet. I never agreed with that "separate" approach to guitar playing. I believe in being a total player with rhythm skills, solo technique, and a well-rounded personal philosophy of the instrument.

Rhythm is one of the most important aspects in music. Any amount of technique simply won't matter if there isn't a flow or "groove" to a solo. Additionally, with scale and arpeggio passages, it's necessary to change the rhythm patterns to avoid sounding too stiff and "formal."

This first exercise uses the country scale (major pentatonic with an added ♭3) in the key of A, and starts with an eighth note pattern that develops into a 16th note pattern and finishes with eighth note triplets. The real key here is to move into each distinctive rhythm pattern smoothly without any discernable "breaks."

TRACK 74   TRACK 75
                  Slow Demo

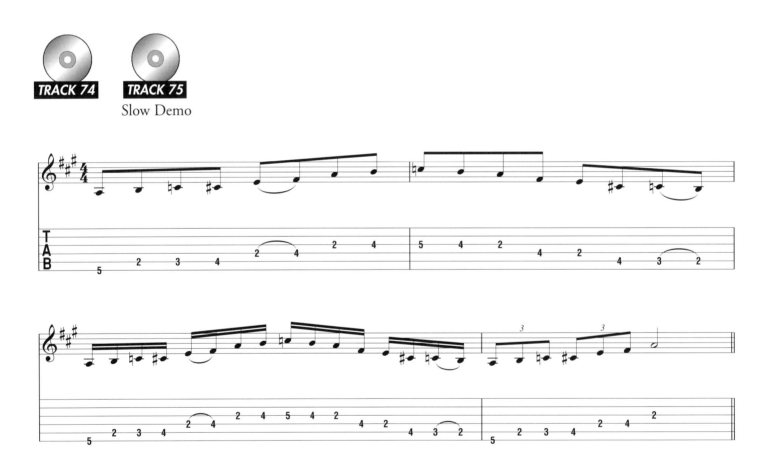

This next exercise is similar to the above, but with a descending scale passage.

TRACK 76 TRACK 77
Slow Demo

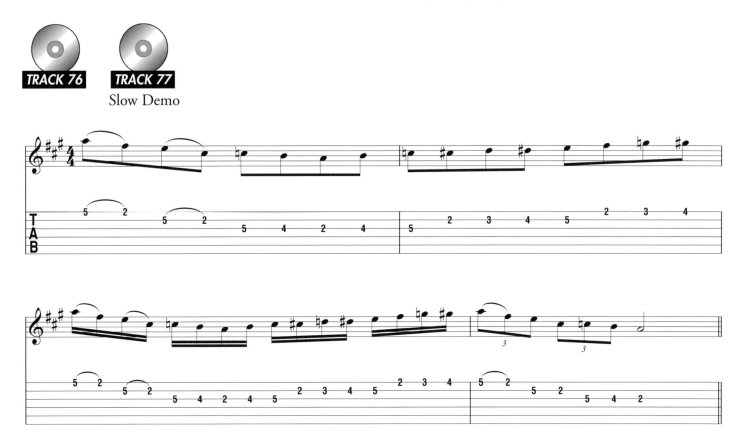

Here's a blues-based lick with exactly the same rhythmic patterns.

TRACK 78 TRACK 79
Slow Demo

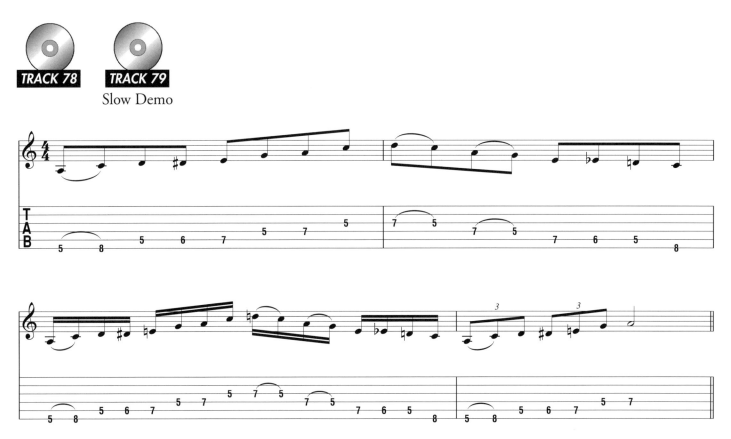

Solo: Rhythm and Grooves

This solo follows the basic I–IV–V changes of a country/blues 12-bar progression with ♭VII added in. Some arpeggio passages contribute spice. Play this slowly at first so you can really feel comfortable with the abrupt rhythmic changes.

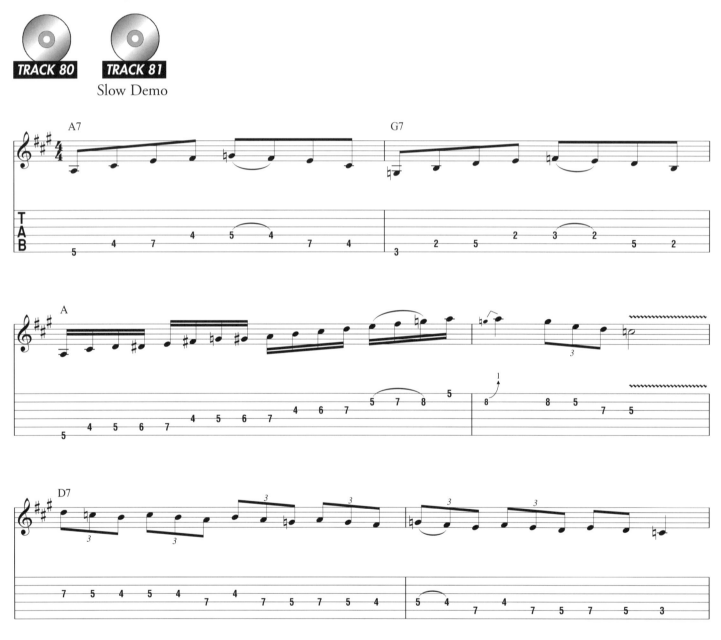

More Seventh Chords

The rhythm technique called *comping* involves simply playing a "backing groove" and covering the chord changes. Set aside your pick (if only temporarily) and use just your fingers to pluck these four-note chord forms so you can get a feel for them. Once these are under your fingers, you should try all of this with your pick.

G7

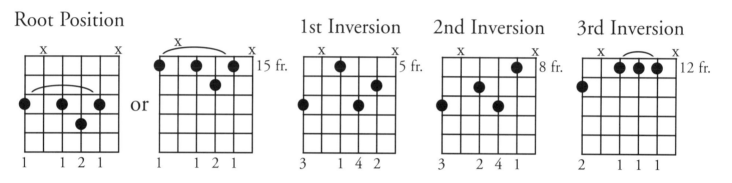

Root Position   or   1st Inversion   2nd Inversion   3rd Inversion

This first exercise explores the root-position form plus the three inversions of the G7 chord. Make sure that each note is equally balanced in volume and tone with the others.

TRACK 82   TRACK 83
Slow Demo

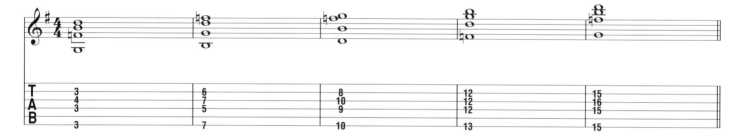

Here are the same inversions with the note durations divided in half. Practice along with the recording to get used to forming these chord shapes.

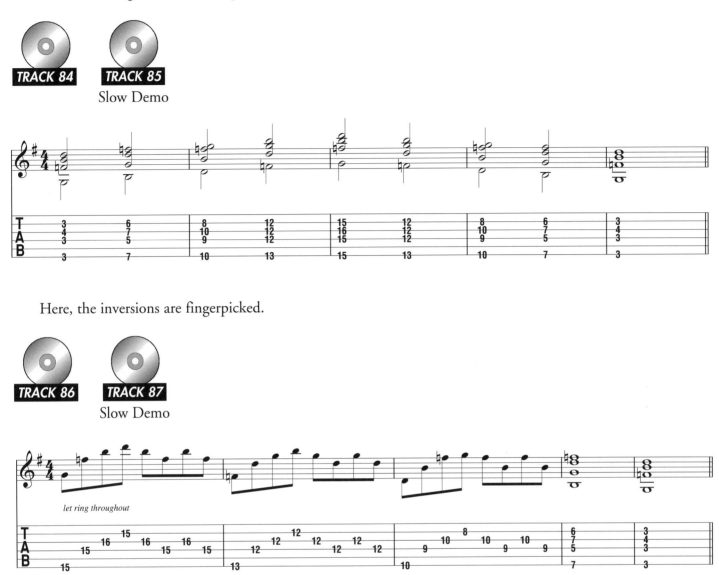

TRACK 84

TRACK 85
Slow Demo

Here, the inversions are fingerpicked.

TRACK 86

TRACK 87
Slow Demo

let ring throughout

Solo: Transition Condition

This solo also follows the basic I–IV–V changes of a country/blues 12-bar progression. Focus on making your chord transitions as smooth as possible. Start out as slowly as you need to and work up to speed.

TRACK 88

TRACK 89
Slow Demo

Country Swing

Swing is not the sole property of jazz—it's equally at home in rockabilly, blues, and especially country. The Brian Setzer Orchestra is a prime example of rockabilly/swing at its finest. For you Texas/swing country music fans, Bob Wills and His Texas Playboys and Asleep at the Wheel are the personifications of this wonderful style of music, and Stevie Ray Vaughn had the blues/swing groove down to a science.

Here's how you can combine certain major pentatonic and blues scales with chromatic passages to create very cool swing passages and melodies. Play the following exercises with as much heart as humanly possible. It's the feel—not the squeal—that makes swing music great!

This first exercise is a blues-based swing lick in the key of G that requires a combination of alternate picking and slurring with hybrid-picked double stops.

TRACK 90   **TRACK 91**
Slow Demo

This next exercise is another blues-based lick that works very nicely for the end of a phrase.

TRACK 92   **TRACK 93**
Slow Demo

Here's yet another killer way to end a swing passage. Pay close attention to the rhythmic changes!

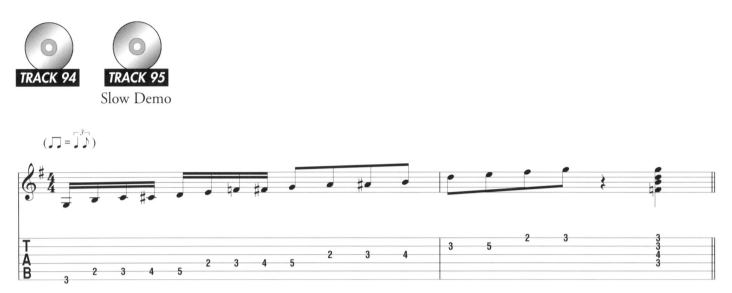

TRACK 94   TRACK 95
Slow Demo

Solo: Dance to the Music

The work on this solo doesn't end when you're simply able to play the notes—it needs to be practiced until you are able to *feel* the rhythmic melodies at any tempo.

TRACK 96   TRACK 97
Slow Demo

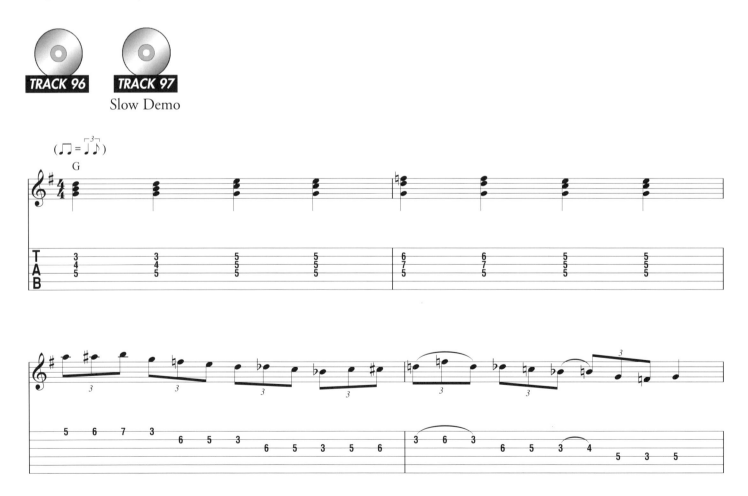

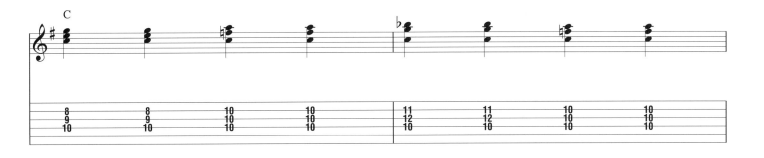

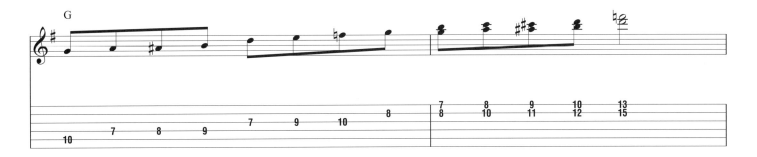

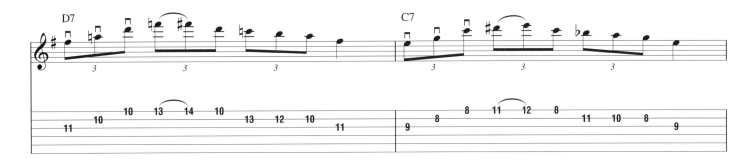

Guitar Notation Legend

Guitar Music can be notated three different ways: on a *musical staff*, in *tablature*, and in *rhythm slashes*.

RHYTHM SLASHES are written above the staff. Strum chords in the rhythm indicated. Use the chord diagrams found at the top of the first page of the transcription for the appropriate chord voicings. Round noteheads indicate single notes.

THE MUSICAL STAFF shows pitches and rhythms and is divided by bar lines into measures. Pitches are named after the first seven letters of the alphabet.

TABLATURE graphically represents the guitar fingerboard. Each horizontal line represents a string, and each number represents a fret.

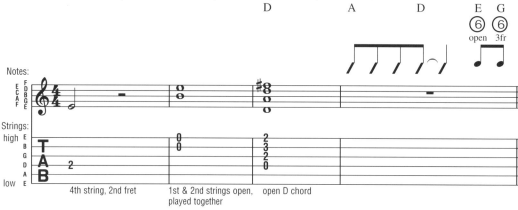

HALF-STEP BEND: Strike the note and bend up 1/2 step.

WHOLE-STEP BEND: Strike the note and bend up one step.

GRACE NOTE BEND: Strike the note and immediately bend up as indicated.

SLIGHT (MICROTONE) BEND: Strike the note and bend up 1/4 step.

BEND AND RELEASE: Strike the note and bend up as indicated, then release back to the original note. Only the first note is struck.

PRE-BEND: Bend the note as indicated, then strike it.

VIBRATO: The string is vibrated by rapidly bending and releasing the note with the fretting hand.

WIDE VIBRATO: The pitch is varied to a greater degree by vibrating with the fretting hand.

HAMMER-ON: Strike the first (lower) note with one finger, then sound the higher note (on the same string) with another finger by fretting it without picking.

PULL-OFF: Place both fingers on the notes to be sounded. Strike the first note and without picking, pull the finger off to sound the second (lower) note.

LEGATO SLIDE: Strike the first note and then slide the same fret-hand finger up or down to the second note. The second note is not struck.

SHIFT SLIDE: Same as legato slide, except the second note is struck.

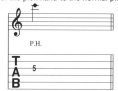

TRILL: Very rapidly alternate between the notes indicated by continuously hammering on and pulling off.

TAPPING: Hammer ("tap") the fret indicated with the pick-hand index or middle finger and pull off to the note fretted by the fret hand.

NATURAL HARMONIC: Strike the note while the fret-hand lightly touches the string directly over the fret indicated.

PINCH HARMONIC: The note is fretted normally and a harmonic is produced by adding the edge of the thumb or the tip of the index finger of the pick hand to the normal pick attack.

PICK SCRAPE: The edge of the pick is rubbed down (or up) the string, producing a scratchy sound.

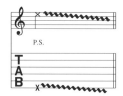

MUFFLED STRINGS: A percussive sound is produced by laying the fret hand across the string(s) without depressing, and striking them with the pick hand.

PALM MUTING: The note is partially muted by the pick hand lightly touching the string(s) just before the bridge.

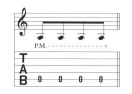

RAKE: Drag the pick across the strings indicated with a single motion.

TREMOLO PICKING: The note is picked as rapidly and continuously as possible.

VIBRATO BAR DIVE AND RETURN: The pitch of the note or chord is dropped a specified number of steps (in rhythm) then returned to the original pitch.

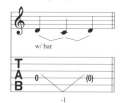

VIBRATO BAR SCOOP: Depress the bar just before striking the note, then quickly release the bar.

VIBRATO BAR DIP: Strike the note and then immediately drop a specified number of steps, then release back to the original pitch.

CHERRY LANE
MUSIC COMPANY

6 East 32nd Street, New York, NY 10016

Quality in Printed Music

The Magazine You Can Play

Visit the Guitar One web site at **www.guitarone.com**

ACOUSTIC INSTRUMENTALISTS
INCLUDES TAB

Over 15 transcriptions from legendary artists such as Leo Kottke, John Fahey, Jorma Kaukonen, Chet Atkins, Adrian Legg, Jeff Beck, and more.

02500399 Play-It-Like-It-Is Guitar..............................$9.95

THE BEST BASS LINES
INCLUDES TAB

24 super songs: Bohemian Rhapsody • Celebrity Skin • Crash Into Me • Crazy Train • Glycerine • Money • November Rain • Smoke on the Water • Sweet Child O' Mine • What Would You Say • You're My Flavor • and more.

02500311 Play-It-Like-It-Is Bass $14.95

BLUES TAB
INCLUDES TAB

14 songs: Boom Boom • Cold Shot • Hide Away • I Can't Quit You Baby • I'm Your Hoochie Coochie Man • In 2 Deep • It Hurts Me Too • Talk to Your Daughter • The Thrill Is Gone • and more.

02500410 Play-It-Like-It-Is Guitar.........................$14.95

CLASSIC ROCK TAB
INCLUDES TAB

15 rock hits: Cat Scratch Fever • Crazy Train • Day Tripper • Hey Joe • Hot Blooded • Start Me Up • We Will Rock You • You Really Got Me • and more.

02500408 Play-It-Like-It-Is Guitar.........................$14.95

MODERN ROCK TAB
INCLUDES TAB

15 of modern rock's best: Are You Gonna Go My Way • Denial • Hanging by a Moment • I Did It • My Hero • Nobody's Real • Rock the Party (Off the Hook) • Shock the Monkey • Slide • Spit It Out • and more.

02500409 Play-It-Like-It-Is Guitar.........................$14.95

SIGNATURE SONGS
INCLUDES TAB

21 artists' trademark hits: Crazy Train (Ozzy Osbourne) • My Generation (The Who) • Smooth (Santana) • Sunshine of Your Love (Cream) • Walk This Way (Aerosmith) • Welcome to the Jungle (Guns N' Roses) • What Would You Say (Dave Matthews Band) • and more.

02500303 Play-It-Like-It-Is Guitar.........................$16.95

BASS SECRETS

WHERE TODAY'S BASS STYLISTS GET TO THE BOTTOM LINE
compiled by John Stix
Bass Secrets brings together 48 columns highlighting specific topics – ranging from the technical to the philosophical – from masters such as Stu Hamm, Randy Coven, Tony Franklin and Billy Sheehan. They cover topics including tapping, walking bass lines, soloing, hand positions, harmonics and more. Clearly illustrated with musical examples.

02500100 ....$12.95

CLASSICS ILLUSTRATED

WHERE BACH MEETS ROCK
by Robert Phillips
Classics Illustrated is designed to demonstrate for readers and players the links between rock and classical music. Each of the 30 columns from *Guitar* highlights one musical concept and provides clear examples in both styles of music. This cool book lets you study moving bass lines over stationary chords in the music of Bach and Guns N' Roses, learn the similarities between "Leyenda" and "Diary of a Madman," and much more!

02500101 ....$9.95

GUITAR SECRETS
INCLUDES TAB

WHERE ROCK'S GUITAR MASTERS SHARE THEIR TRICKS, TIPS & TECHNIQUES
compiled by John Stix
This unique and informative compilation features 42 columns culled from *Guitar* magazine. Readers will discover dozens of techniques and playing tips, and gain practical advice and words of wisdom from guitar masters.

02500099 ....$10.95

IN THE LISTENING ROOM

WHERE ARTISTS CRITIQUE THE MUSIC OF THEIR PEERS
compiled by John Stix
A compilation of 75 columns from *Guitar* magazine, *In the Listening Room* provides a unique opportunity for readers to hear major recording artists remark on the music of their peers. These artists were given no information about what they would hear, and their comments often tell as much about themselves as they do about the music they listened to. Includes candid critiques by music legends like Aerosmith, Jeff Beck, Jack Bruce, Dimebag Darrell, Buddy Guy, Kirk Hammett, Eric Johnson, John McLaughlin, Dave Navarro, Carlos Santana, Joe Satriani, Stevie Ray Vaughan, and many others.

02500097 ....$14.95

EXCLUSIVELY DISTRIBUTED BY

HAL•LEONARD®
CORPORATION

7777 W. BLUEMOUND RD. P.O. BOX 13819 MILWAUKEE, WI 53213

LEGENDS OF LEAD GUITAR

THE BEST OF INTERVIEWS: 1995-2000
This is a fascinating compilation of interviews with today's greatest guitarists! From deeply rooted blues giants to the most fearless pioneers, legendary players reveal how they achieve their extraordinary craft.

02500329 ....$14.95

LESSON LAB

This exceptional book/CD pack features more than 20 in-depth lessons. Tackle in detail a variety of pertinent music- and guitar-related subjects, such as scales, chords, theory, guitar technique, songwriting, and much more!

02500330 Book/CD Pack......................................$19.95

NOISE & FEEDBACK

THE BEST OF 1995-2000: YOUR QUESTIONS ANSWERED
If you ever wanted to know about a specific guitar lick, trick, technique or effect, this book/CD pack is for you! It features over 70 lessons on composing • computer assistance • education and career advice • equipment • technique • terminology and notation • tunings • and more.

02500328 Book/CD Pack......................................$17.95

OPEN EARS

A JOURNEY THROUGH LIFE WITH GUITAR IN HAND
by Steve Morse
In this collection of 50 *Guitar* magazine columns from the mid-'90s on, guitarist Steve Morse sets the story straight about what being a working musician *really* means. He deals out practical advice on: playing with the band, songwriting, recording and equipment, and more, through anecdotes of his hard-knock lessons learned.

02500333 ....$10.95

SPOTLIGHT ON STYLE

THE BEST OF 1995-2000: AN EXPLORER'S GUIDE TO GUITAR
This book and CD cover 18 of the world's most popular guitar styles, including: blues guitar • classical guitar • country guitar • funk guitar • jazz guitar • Latin guitar • metal • rockabilly and more!

02500320 Book/CD Pack......................................$19.95

STUDIO CITY

PROFESSIONAL SESSION RECORDING FOR GUITARISTS
by Carl Verheyen
In this collection of colomns from Guitar Magazine, guitarists will learn how to: exercise studio etiquette and act professionally • acquire, assemble and set up gear for sessions • use the tricks of the trade to become a studio hero • get repeat call-backs • and more.

02500195 ....$9.95

More Great Piano/Vocal Books

FROM CHERRY LANE

For a complete listing of Cherry Lane titles available,
including contents listings, please visit our web site at
www.cherrylane.com

02500343	Almost Famous	$14.95
02502171	The Best of Boston	$17.95
02500672	Black Eyed Peas – Elephunk	$17.95
02500665	Sammy Cahn Songbook	$24.95
02500144	Mary Chapin Carpenter – Party Doll & Other Favorites	$16.95
02502163	Mary Chapin Carpenter – Stones in the Road	$17.95
02502165	John Denver Anthology – Revised.	$22.95
02502227	John Denver – A Celebration of Life	$14.95
02500002	John Denver Christmas	$14.95
02502166	John Denver's Greatest Hits	$17.95
02502151	John Denver – A Legacy in Song (Softcover)	$24.95
02502152	John Denver – A Legacy in Song (Hardcover)	$34.95
02500566	Poems, Prayers and Promises: The Art and Soul of John Denver	$19.95
02500326	John Denver – The Wildlife Concert	$17.95
02500501	John Denver and the Muppets: A Christmas Together	$9.95
02509922	The Songs of Bob Dylan	$29.95
02500586	Linda Eder – Broadway My Way	$14.95
02500497	Linda Eder – Gold	$14.95
02500396	Linda Eder – Christmas Stays the Same	$17.95
02500175	Linda Eder – It's No Secret Anymore	$14.95
02502209	Linda Eder – It's Time	$17.95
02500630	Donald Fagen – 5 of the Best	$7.95
02500535	Erroll Garner Anthology	$19.95
02500270	Gilbert & Sullivan for Easy Piano	$12.95
02500318	Gladiator	$12.95
02500273	Gold & Glory: The Road to El Dorado	$16.95
02502126	Best of Guns N' Roses	$17.95
02502072	Guns N' Roses – Selections from Use Your Illusion I and II	$17.95
02500014	Sir Roland Hanna Collection	$19.95
02500352	Hanson – This Time Around	$16.95
02502134	Best of Lenny Kravitz	$12.95
02500012	Lenny Kravitz – 5	$16.95
02500381	Lenny Kravitz – Greatest Hits	$14.95
02503701	Man of La Mancha	$10.95

02500693	Dave Matthews – Some Devil	$16.95
02500555	Dave Matthews Band – Busted Stuff	$16.95
02500003	Dave Matthews Band – Before These Crowded Streets	$17.95
02502199	Dave Matthews Band – Crash	$17.95
02500390	Dave Matthews Band – Everyday	$14.95
02500493	Dave Matthews Band – Live in Chicago 12/19/98 at the United Center	$14.95
02502192	Dave Matthews Band – Under the Table and Dreaming	$17.95
02500681	John Mayer – Heavier Things	$16.95
02500563	John Mayer – Room for Squares	$16.95
02500081	Natalie Merchant – Ophelia	$14.95
02500423	Natalie Merchant – Tigerlily	$14.95
02502895	Nine	$17.95
02500425	Time and Love: The Art and Soul of Laura Nyro	$19.95
02502204	The Best of Metallica	$17.95
02500407	O-Town	$14.95
02500010	Tom Paxton – The Honor of Your Company	$17.95
02507962	Peter, Paul & Mary – Holiday Concert	$17.95
02500145	Pokemon 2.B.A. Master	$12.95
02500026	The Prince of Egypt	$16.95
02500660	Best of Bonnie Raitt	$17.95
02502189	The Bonnie Raitt Collection	$22.95
02502230	Bonnie Raitt – Fundamental	$17.95
02502139	Bonnie Raitt – Longing in Their Hearts	$16.95
02502088	Bonnie Raitt – Luck of the Draw	$14.95
02507958	Bonnie Raitt – Nick of Time	$14.95
02502190	Bonnie Raitt – Road Tested	$24.95
02502218	Kenny Rogers – The Gift	$16.95
02500072	Saving Private Ryan	$14.95
02500197	SHeDAISY – The Whole SHeBANG	$14.95
02500414	Shrek	$14.95
02500536	Spirit – Stallion of the Cimarron	$16.95
02500166	Steely Dan – Anthology	$17.95
02500622	Steely Dan – Everything Must Go	$14.95
02500284	Steely Dan – Two Against Nature	$14.95
02500165	Best of Steely Dan	$14.95

02500344	Billy Strayhorn: An American Master	$17.95
02502132	Barbra Streisand – Back to Broadway	$19.95
02500515	Barbra Streisand – Christmas Memories	$16.95
02507969	Barbra Streisand – A Collection: Greatest Hits and More	$17.95
02502164	Barbra Streisand – The Concert	$22.95
02500550	Essential Barbra Streisand	$24.95
02502228	Barbra Streisand – Higher Ground	$16.95
02500196	Barbra Streisand – A Love Like Ours	$16.95
02500280	Barbra Streisand – Timeless	$19.95
02503617	John Tesh – Avalon	$15.95
02502178	The John Tesh Collection	$17.95
02503623	John Tesh – A Family Christmas	$15.95
02505511	John Tesh – Favorites for Easy Piano	$12.95
02503630	John Tesh – Grand Passion	$16.95
02500124	John Tesh – One World	$14.95
02500307	John Tesh – Pure Movies 2	$16.95
02500565	Thoroughly Modern Millie	$17.95
02500576	Toto – 5 of the Best	$7.95
02502175	Tower of Power – Silver Anniversary	$17.95
02502198	The "Weird Al" Yankovic Anthology	$17.95
02502217	Trisha Yearwood – A Collection of Hits	$16.95
02500334	Maury Yeston – December Songs	$17.95
02502225	The Maury Yeston Songbook	$19.95

See your local music dealer or contact:

CHERRY LANE MUSIC COMPANY
6 East 32nd Street, New York, NY 10016
Quality in Printed Music

EXCLUSIVELY DISTRIBUTED BY

HAL•LEONARD®
CORPORATION
7777 W. BLUEMOUND RD. P.O. BOX 13819 MILWAUKEE, WI 53213

Prices, contents and availability subject to change without notice.

0404

great songs series

Cherry Lane Music is proud to present this legendary series which has delighted players and performers for generations.

Great Songs of the Fifties

The latest release in Cherry Lane's acclaimed Great Songs series, this songbook presents 51 musical memories from the fabulous '50s! Features rock, pop, country, Broadway and movie tunes, including: All Shook Up • At the Hop • Blue Suede Shoes • Dream Lover • Fly Me to the Moon • Kansas City • Love Me Tender • Misty • Peggy Sue • Rock Around the Clock • Sea of Love • Sixteen Tons • Take the "A" Train • Wonderful! Wonderful! • and more. Includes an introduction by award-winning journalist Bruce Pollock.

_____02500323 P/V/G.............................$16.95

Great Songs of the Sixties, Vol. 1 – Revised Edition

The newly updated version of this classic book includes 80 faves from the 1960s: Angel of the Morning • Bridge over Troubled Water • Cabaret • Different Drum • Do You Believe in Magic • Eve of Destruction • Georgy Girl • It Was a Very Good Year • Monday, Monday • People • Spinning Wheel • Walk on By • and more.

_____02509902 P/V/G.............................$19.95

Great Songs of the Sixties, Vol. 2 – Revised Edition

61 more 60s hits: And When I Die • California Dreamin' • Crying • The 59th Street Bridge Song (Feelin' Groovy) • For Once in My Life • Honey • Little Green Apples • MacArthur Park • Me and Bobby McGee • Nowhere Man • Piece of My Heart • Sugar, Sugar • You Made Me So Very Happy • and more.

_____02509904 P/V/G.............................$19.95

Great Songs of the Seventies – Revised Edition

This super collection of 70 big hits from the '70s includes: After the Love Has Gone • Afternoon Delight • Annie's Song • Band on the Run • Cold as Ice • FM • Imagine • It's Too Late • Layla • Let It Be • Maggie May • Piano Man • Shelter from the Storm • Superstar • Sweet Baby James • Time in a Bottle • The Way We Were • more!

_____02509917 P/V/G.............................$19.95

Prices, contents, and availability subject to change without notice.

Great Songs of the Seventies – Volume 2

Features 58 outstanding '70s songs in rock, pop, country, Broadway and movie genres: American Woman • Baby, I'm-A Want You • Day by Day • Do That to Me One More Time • Dog & Butterfly • Don't Cry Out Loud • Dreamboat Annie • Follow Me • Get Closer • Grease • Heard It in a Love Song • I'll Be There • It's a Heartache • The Loco-Motion • My Eyes Adored You • New Kid in Town • Night Fever • On and On • Sing • Summer Breeze • Tonight's the Night • We Are the Champions • Y.M.C.A. • and more. Includes articles by Cherry Lane Music Company founder Milt Okun, and award-winning music journalist Bruce Pollock.

_____02500322 P/V/G.............................$19.95

Great Songs of the Eighties – Revised Edition

This newly revised edition features 50 songs in rock, pop & country styles, plus hits from Broadway and the movies! Songs: Almost Paradise • Angel of the Morning • Do You Really Want to Hurt Me • Endless Love • Flashdance...What a Feeling • Guilty • Hungry Eyes • (Just Like) Starting Over • Let Love Rule • Missing You • Patience • Through the Years • Time After Time • Total Eclipse of the Heart • and more.

_____02502125 P/V/G.............................$18.95

Great Songs of the Nineties

This terrific collection features 48 big hits in many styles. Includes: Achy Breaky Heart • Beautiful in My Eyes • Believe • Black Hole Sun • Black Velvet • Blaze of Glory • Building a Mystery • Crash into Me • Fields of Gold • From a Distance • Glycerine • Here and Now • Hold My Hand • I'll Make Love to You • Ironic • Linger • My Heart Will Go On • Waterfalls • Wonderwall • and more.

_____02500040 P/V/G.............................$16.95

Great Songs of the Pop Era

Over 50 hits from the pop era, including: Amazed • Annie's Song • Ebony and Ivory • Every Breath You Take • Hey Nineteen • I Want to Know What Love Is • I'm Every Woman • Just the Two of Us • Leaving on a Jet Plane • My Cherie Amour • Raindrops Keep Fallin' on My Head • Rocky Mountain High • This Is the Moment • Time After Time • (I've Had) the Time of My Life • What a Wonderful World • and more!

_____02500043 Easy Piano $16.95

CHERRY LANE
MUSIC COMPANY
6 East 32nd Street, New York, NY 10016
Quality in Printed Music

Visit Cherry Lane on the Internet at
www.cherrylane.com

EXCLUSIVELY DISTRIBUTED BY

HAL•LEONARD®
CORPORATION
7777 W. BLUEMOUND RD. P.O. BOX 13819 MILWAUKEE, WI 53213

THE HOTTEST TAB SONGBOOKS AVAILABLE FOR GUITAR & BASS!

PLAY IT LIKE IT IS GUITAR WITH TABLATURE
NOTE-FOR-NOTE TRANSCRIPTIONS

PLAY IT LIKE IT IS BASS WITH TABLATURE
NOTE-FOR-NOTE TRANSCRIPTIONS

from

CHERRY LANE MUSIC COMPANY

Quality in Printed Music

Guitar Transcriptions

02500593	**Best of Ryan Adams**	$19.95
02500443	Alien Ant Farm – ANThology	$19.95
02501272	Bush – 16 Stone	$21.95
02500193	Bush – The Science of Things	$19.95
02500098	Coal Chamber	$19.95
02500174	Coal Chamber – Chamber Music	$19.95
02500179	Mary Chapin Carpenter – Authentic Guitar Style of	$16.95
02500132	Evolution of Fear Factory	$19.95
02500198	Best of Foreigner	$19.95
02501242	Guns N' Roses – Anthology	$24.95
02506953	Guns N' Roses – Appetite for Destruction	$22.95
02501286	Guns N' Roses Complete, Volume 1	$24.95
02501287	Guns N' Roses Complete, Volume 2	$24.95
02506211	Guns N' Roses – 5 of the Best, Vol. 1	$12.95
02506975	Guns N' Roses – GN'R Lies	$19.95
02500299	Guns N' Roses – Live Era '87-'93 Highlights	$24.95
02501193	Guns N' Roses – Use Your Illusion I	$24.95
02501194	Guns N' Roses – Use Your Illusion II	$24.95
02500458	**Best of Warren Haynes**	$19.95
02500387	Best of Heart	$19.95
02500007	Hole – Celebrity Skin	$19.95
02501260	Hole – Live Through This	$19.95
02500516	**Jimmy Eat World**	$19.95
02500554	**Jack Johnson – Brushfire Fairytales**	$19.95
02500380	Lenny Kravitz – Greatest Hits	$19.95
02500469	**Lenny Kravitz – Lenny**	$19.95
02500024	Best of Lenny Kravitz	$19.95
02500375	Lifehouse – No Name Face	$19.95
02500558	**Lifehouse – Stanley Climbfall**	$19.95
02500362	Best of Little Feat	$19.95
02501259	Machine Head – Burn My Eyes	$19.95
02500173	Machine Head – The Burning Red	$19.95
02500305	Best of The Marshall Tucker Band	$19.95
02501357	Dave Matthews Band – Before These Crowded Streets	$19.95
02500553	**Dave Matthews Band – Busted Stuff**	$22.95
02501279	Dave Matthews Band – Crash	$19.95
02500389	Dave Matthews Band – Everyday	$19.95
02500488	**Dave Matthews Band – Live in Chicago 12/19/98 at the United Center, Vol. 1**	$19.95
02500489	**Dave Matthews Band – Live in Chicago 12/19/98 at the United Center, Vol. 2**	$19.95
02501266	Dave Matthews Band – Under the Table and Dreaming	$19.95
02500131	Dave Matthews/Tim Reynolds – Live at Luther College, Vol. 1	$19.95
02500611	Dave Matthews/Tim Reynolds – Live at Luther College, Vol. 2	$19.95
02500529	**John Mayer – Room for Squares**	$19.95
02506965	Metallica – ...And Justice for All	$22.95
02506210	Metallica – 5 of the Best/Vol.1	$12.95
02506235	Metallica – 5 of the Best/Vol. 2	$12.95
02500070	Metallica – Garage, Inc.	$24.95
02507018	Metallica – Kill 'Em All	$19.95
02501232	Metallica – Live: Binge & Purge	$19.95
02501275	Metallica – Load	$24.95
02507920	Metallica – Master of Puppets	$19.95
02501195	Metallica – Metallica	$22.95
02501297	Metallica – ReLoad	$24.95
02507019	Metallica – Ride the Lightning	$19.95
02500279	Metallica – S&M Highlights	$24.95
02500577	**Molly Hatchet – 5 of the Best**	$9.95
02501353	Best of Steve Morse	$19.95
02500448	**Best of Ted Nugent**	$19.95
02500348	Ozzy Osbourne – Blizzard of Ozz	$19.95
02501277	Ozzy Osbourne – Diary of a Madman	$19.95
02509973	Ozzy Osbourne – Songbook	$24.95
02507904	Ozzy Osbourne/Randy Rhoads Tribute	$22.95
02500316	Papa Roach – Infest	$19.95
02500545	**Papa Roach – Lovehatetragedy**	$19.95
02500194	Powerman 5000 – Tonight the Stars Revolt!	$17.95
02500025	Primus Anthology – A-N (Guitar/Bass)	$19.95
02500091	Primus Anthology – O-Z (Guitar/Bass)	$19.95
02500468	**Primus – Sailing the Seas of Cheese**	$19.95
02500508	**Bonnie Raitt – Silver Lining**	$19.95
02501268	Joe Satriani	$22.95
02501299	Joe Satriani – Crystal Planet	$24.95
02500306	Joe Satriani – Engines of Creation	$22.95
02501205	Joe Satriani – The Extremist	$22.95
02507029	Joe Satriani – Flying in a Blue Dream	$22.95
02507074	Joe Satriani – Not of This Earth	$19.95
02500544	**Joe Satriani – Strange Beautiful Music**	$19.95
02506959	Joe Satriani – Surfing with the Alien	$19.95
02501226	Joe Satriani – Time Machine 1	$19.95
02500560	**Joe Satriani Anthology**	$24.95
02501255	Best of Joe Satriani	$19.95
02500088	Sepultura – Against	$19.95
02501239	Sepultura – Arise	$19.95
02501240	Sepultura – Beneath the Remains	$19.95
02501238	Sepultura – Chaos A.D.	$19.95
02500188	Best of the Brian Setzer Orchestra	$19.95
02500177	Sevendust	$19.95
02500176	Sevendust – Home	$19.95
02500090	Soulfly	$19.95
02501230	Soundgarden – Superunknown	$19.95
02501250	Best of Soundgarden	$19.95
02500168	Steely Dan's Greatest Songs	$19.95
02500167	Best of Steely Dan for Guitar	$19.95
02501263	Tesla – Time's Making Changes	$19.95
02500583	**The White Stripes – White Blood Cells**	$19.95
02500431	Best of Johnny Winter	$19.95
02500199	Best of Zakk Wylde	$22.95
02500517	**WWE – Forceable Entry**	$19.95
02500104	**WWF: The Music, Vol.3**	$19.95

Bass Transcriptions

02500008	Best of Bush	$16.95
02505920	Bush – 16 Stone	$19.95
02506966	Guns N' Roses – Appetite for Destruction	$19.95
02500504	**Best of Guns N' Roses for Bass**	$14.95
02500013	Best of The Dave Matthews Band	$17.95
02505911	Metallica – Metallica	$19.95
02506982	Metallica – ...And Justice for All	$19.95
02500075	Metallica – Garage, Inc.	$24.95
02507039	Metallica – Kill 'Em All	$19.95
02505919	Metallica – Load	$19.95
02506961	Metallica – Master of Puppets	$19.95
02505926	Metallica – ReLoad	$21.95
02507040	Metallica – Ride the Lightning	$17.95
02500288	Metallica – S&M Highlights	$19.95
02500347	**Papa Roach – Infest**	$17.95
02500539	**Sittin' In with Rocco Prestia of Tower of Power**	$19.95
02500025	Primus Anthology – A-N (Guitar/Bass)	$19.95
02500091	Primus Anthology – O-Z (Guitar/Bass)	$19.95
02500500	**Best of Joe Satriani for Bass**	$14.95
02500317	**Victor Wooten Songbook**	$19.95

Transcribed Scores

02500361	**Guns N' Roses Greatest Hits**	$24.95
02500282	**Lenny Kravitz – Greatest Hits**	$24.95
02500496	**Lenny Kravitz – Lenny**	$24.95
02500424	**Best of Metallica**	$24.95
02500283	**Joe Satriani – Greatest Hits**	$24.95

FOR MORE INFORMATION, SEE YOUR LOCAL MUSIC DEALER, OR WRITE TO:

HAL•LEONARD® CORPORATION

7777 W. BLUEMOUND RD. P.O. BOX 13819 MILWAUKEE, WI 53213

Prices, contents and availability subject to change without notice.

0303